Hungry for Math:

Poems to Munch On

Text © 2015 Kari-Lynn Winters & Lori Sherritt-Fleming
Illustrations © 2015 Peggy Collins

Published in Canada in 2015 by Fitzhenry & Whiteside, 195 Allstate Parkway, Markham, ON, L3R 4T8 www.fitzhenry.ca
Published in the U.S. in 2015 by Fitzhenry & Whiteside, 311 Washington Street, Brighton, Massachusetts 02135

5 4 3 2 1

We acknowledge with thanks the Canada Council for the Arts, and the Ontario Arts Council for their support of our publishing program.
We acknowledge the financial support of the Government of Canada through the Canada Book Fund (CBF) for our publishing activities.

Library and Archives Canada Cataloguing in Publication
Winters, Kari-Lynn, 1969-, author
Hungry for math : poems to munch on / Kari-Lynn Winters & Lori
Sherritt-Fleming ; illustrated by Peggy Collins.
Issued in print and electronic formats.
ISBN 978-1-55455-307-5 (bound).—ISBN 978-1-55455-863-6 (pdf)
1. Mathematics--Juvenile poetry. 2. Children's poetry, Canadian
(English). I. Sherritt-Fleming, Lori, 1968-, author II. Collins, Peggy,
illustrator III. Title.
PS8645.I5745H85 2015   jC811'.6   C2014-906728-3
C2014-906729-1

Publisher Cataloging-in-Publication Data (U.S.)
Winters, Kari-Lynn, 1969-
Hungry for math : poems to munch on / Kari-Lynn Winters and Lori Sherritt-Fleming ; illustrated by Peggy Collins.
[32] pages : color illustrations ; cm.
Also published in electronic format.
Summary: A collection of fun and educational poems illustrating various math concepts, including shapes, patterns, symmetry, skip-counting, money, time, and ordinal numbers.

ISBN-13: 978-1-55455-307-5
ISBN-13: 978-1-55455-863-6 (ePDF)

1. Mathematics – Juvenile poetry. 2. Children's poetry, Canadian (English). I. Sherritt-Fleming, Lori, 1968- . II. Collins, Peggy. III. Title.
811.6 dc23   PR9199.4W458H85   2015

Tiffany Stone + Scot Ritchie + Christie Harkin + Cathy Sandusky = Team members who counted us in and who were and still are invaluable. —K-L. W.
For Mike, Aidan and Dylan who tirelessly searched for rot-TEN dragons behind the couch at Grandma and Grandpa's and for Lily, Maya and Ava my favourite wee Spendosaurs. —L. S-F.
For my little spendosaurs, MO & Z. xo —P.C.

Text and cover design by Kerry Designs
Cover illustration courtesy of Peggy Collins
Printed and bound in China by Sheck Wah Tong Printing Press Ltd.

Hungry for Math:
Poems to Munch On

Kari-Lynn Winters & Lori Sherritt-Fleming
Illustrated by Peggy Collins

Fitzhenry & Whiteside

Hungry for Math

He was hungry for math,
always ready to munch.
Math for his breakfast,
math for his lunch.

He'd pig out on pie charts
and bar graphs galore,
binge on skip-counting,
and still ask for more.

Shapes — he discovered —
were less filling fare.
He'd taste test a rhombus,
sparing room for a square.

He'd devour the dollars
atop his dessert,
then slurp on the coins
he'd slopped on his shirt.

At night, in the dark,
he'd gnaw on base ten,
toss back some clocks,
and crunch numbers again.

The Balanced Bee

Three circles, tall not wide.
Six legs — three per side.
Two plus two wings, on its back.
Bands of yellow, white, and black.
Compound eyes to spy the view.
Antennae, not one — always two.
Now fold your paper.
It's plain to see.
Bees are balanced.
It's symmetry!

Patterns Rock!

Rat-a tat. Rat-a-tat. Rat-a-tat. BANG!
Rat-a-tat. Rat-a-tat. Rat-a-tat. BANG!

Bang out your patterns.
Smash them out loud.
You're rhythm-masters. You rock the crowd!

Strum-a-THRUM. Strum-a-THRUM. Twang-ity-TWANG.
Strum-a-THRUM. Strum-a-THRUM. Twang-ity-TWANG.

Cut loose with patterns.
You're super stars,
blasting out tunes on electric guitars!

Rat-a tat. Rat-a-tat. Rat-a-tat. BANG!
Strum-a-THRUM. Strum-a-THRUM. Twang-ity-TWANG.

Drumming and strumming,
what a grand start.
Now paint the town with your musical art!

The Shape of Things

Find them all.
Name and compare.
2-D shapes are everywhere.

In the wild—
hey, why not?
Triangle tooth and
trapezoid spot.

Up in trees?
There's a sight!
Hexagon treat and rhombus kite.

Under the sea,
there they are.
Oval shell and five-point star.

At the farm,
in disguise—
circle snout and rectangle eyes.

This shape here.
That shape there.
2-D shapes are everywhere!

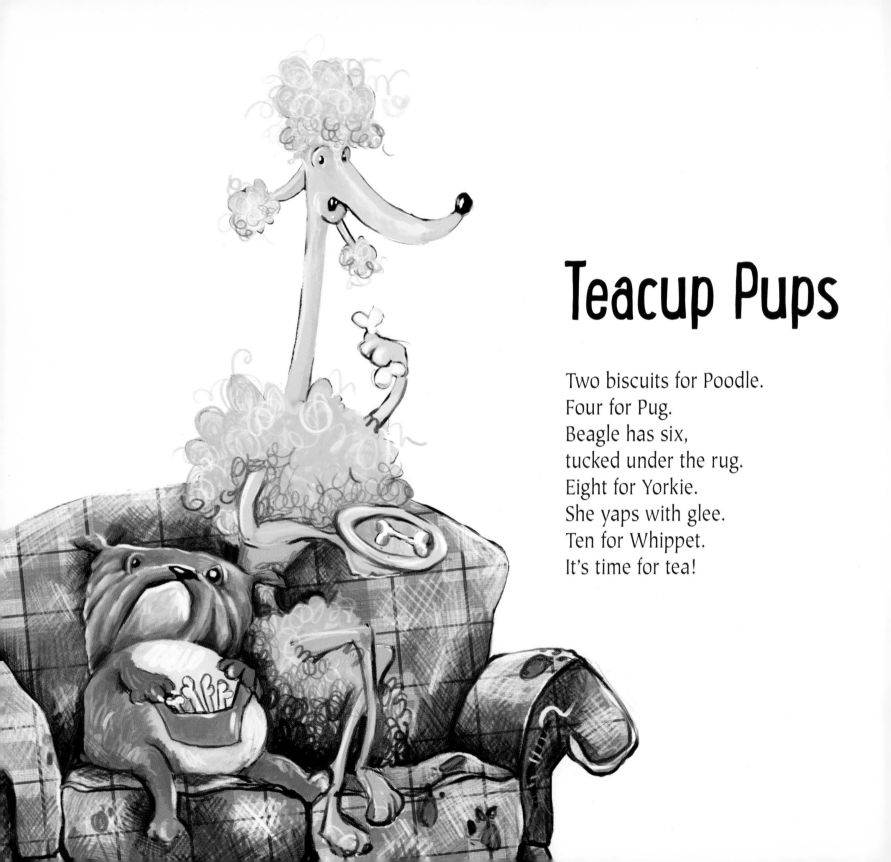

Teacup Pups

Two biscuits for Poodle.
Four for Pug.
Beagle has six,
tucked under the rug.
Eight for Yorkie.
She yaps with glee.
Ten for Whippet.
It's time for tea!

Rot–TEN Dragons

Look *very* closely.
When they think you've left home,
count fifty rot-TEN dragons
sneaking out to roam.

TEN slide down the chimney,
whooshing through the grime.
You'll hear them calling,
"Hey, it's PARTY time!"

Swimming in the toilet,
diving in the tub,
TEN more splashing dragons
rub-a-dub and scrub!

Hockey in the hallway,
scraping up the floor,
TEN more rot-TEN players
shoot…and score!

Racing through the office,
riding scooter bikes.
TEN more granny dragons
zoom along…yikes!

"People are coming!"
TEN more call and hack.
All fifty dragons hustle,
cleaning up the shack!

Look *very* closely.
(they know you're home again).
Count fifty hiding dragons
in five groups of ten.

Aye, me name is Pirate O'Greaves,
I coverz me treas-ARRH
with banana leaves.

I eyez the plant and then the gap,
I countz to me self,
and beginz me rap:

"Before I climbz this blasted weed,
how many leaflets does I need?
Seven?
Eleven?
Twenty-two?
How many leaflets must I strew
over this treas-ARRH,
ontoppa this pit,
so me mateys can't spyz it?"

Help me now—guess and measure—
the number of leaves that coverz me treas-ARRH.

The Spendosaur

Spendosaur, Spendosaur,
hear him ROAR,
thundering down to the candy store.
He's got money he wants to spend
on treats to share with his
Spendosaur friend.

One penny buys a chocolate-dipped pickle.
He orders five and pays with a nickel.

Ten pennies, he knows, add up to a dime
for gumdrops smothered in swampy slime.

Twenty-five pennies
make a quarter to pay
for Spendosaur gloppy-plops
that last all day.

One hundred pennies left.
He just can't stop.
With his very last dollar,
he buys...THE SHOP!

Spendosaur, Spendosaur, hear him ROAR,
thundering away with the candy store.
He's spent his last penny and it's no joke,
his dino-bank is empty… and now
he's broke.

That Kitty Counts

Twelve treats for Chantilly,
who never acts silly
when she is hosting a party.

Burmese eats fourteen,
then licks his fur clean.
(He likes to look like a smartie.)

In struts Bombay,
with plenty to say.
He gobbles down sixteen more.

Eighteen for Korat,
a hardy grey cat.
She sneaks hers out the back door.

Miss Havana Brown,
the sleekest in town,
purrrrrs, "I think you've all had plenty."

She then, with a clatter,
lays claim to the platter,
and scarfs down the final twenty.

Move Around The Clock

Hickory dickory dock.
The mouse ran up the clock.
The clock struck one...
But the mouse wasn't done.
Hickory dickory dock.

2 o'clock sprint.

3 o'clock hop.

4:30 skitter—I'll never stop!

7 o'clock climb.

8 o'clock prance.

9:30 jump—SQUEAK! Shake and danc

10 o'clock squirm.

11 o'clock leap.

Noon...*yawn*. I need to sleep.

So glad I made it. Hickory hooray!

Huh? I'm not finished...
a 24-hour day?
Right...*yawn* ...okay...zzz.

Hickory dickory done.
The mouse, too tired to run,
fell fast asleep,
didn't make a peep.
Hickory dickory done.

It All ADDS Up

Zoe's has a ribbon.
Chad's has flaps.
Tyla sports a toque.
The twins have caps.

Sue's has pom-poms.
Finn's has an arrow.
Brie wears a bonnet.
José—a sombrero.

But where is my hat?
I guess I'll have to face it.
It's gone! It's missing!
I know I can't replace it!

Mine has ribbons
and a pom-pom upon it,
but it doesn't have flaps...
or look like Brie's bonnet.

My hat's not a cap.
It's not a straw sombrero.
It's not a cozy toque,
and it doesn't have an arrow.

My hat is wool and plaid.
It's shaped like half a clam!
Tyla calls it funny,
but I call it my TAM.

Soap Box First

The soapbox derby is all about speed.
A first-rate car is what you need.

3,2,1…Go!

In fifth place, we had to swerve.
We almost crashed, but made the curve.

In fourth place, SMASH-BANG-THUMP!
We caught some air as we hit a bump.

In third place, we skidded and slipped,
speeding so fast we almost flipped.

In second place, RUMBLE-SQUEAL!
Over the hill, we lost our wheel.

In first place, through a metal spray.
We won the race! Yippee! Hooray!

More About Math

Bar graph: a visual display that uses bars of different heights to measure data (information).

Base Ten: a math tool used to identify place value, and to count and compare whole numbers up to 1000.

Estimating: a mental math activity where a person makes his or her best guess about quantity (how many) or value (how much) based on information that is known.

Hexagon: this six-sided, two-dimensional shape can sometimes look like a honeycomb.

Logical reasoning: solving a puzzle or answering a question using clues.

Ordinal numbers: numbers that define a position in a series (e.g., first, second, third).

Pie chart: a circular graph that uses pie-shaped slices to measure data (information).

Place Value: the value of a number based on its position. For example, the 5 in 53 = 5 tens, and the 3 = 3 ones.

Rhombus: this four-sided, two-dimensional shape has opposite sides that are parallel and equal, and can sometimes look like a diamond.

Skip Counting: counting in intervals other than one (e.g., counting by fives—5, 10, 15).

Symmetry: when one half of a picture mirrors its other half.

Trapezoid: this four-sided, two-dimensional shape has one pair of parallel sides and sometimes looks like a triangle with the top cut off.